Long, Long ago in Jerusalem

The life and resurrection of Jesus

Long, Long ago in Jerusalem

The life and resurrection of Jesus

Told by Carine Mackenzie

Illustrated by Fred Apps

Published by Christian Focus Publications

© 2001 Christian Focus Publications Ltd
Geanies House, Fearn,
Tain, Ross-shire IV20 1TW
www.christianfocus.com

Illustrations by Fred Apps
Written by Carine Mackenzie
ISBN 1-85792-390-1

Long, long ago, in the city of Jerusalem a great many exciting and amazing things happened... because Jesus was there!

He performed miracles and healed the sick throughout the whole city. He said many amazing things as well. Some people believed him and followed him - some people didn't like what he said at all and caused trouble for him. However, Jesus, God's Son, was there in Jerusalem for a reason. God had a plan - a plan of salvation - and Jesus was crucial to this plan.

As Jesus lived and worked in the dusty streets of Jerusalem he met people, helped them, loved them and spoke to them about the exciting mysteries of the Kingdom of God. But very many people refused to believe him and one day, as he approached Jerusalem and saw the city, he wept over it. Jesus longed for these people to turn from their sin and love God. He longs for you to do the same.

'O Jerusalem, Jerusalem...
how often I have longed
to gather your children
together, as a hen gathers her
chicks under her wings, but
you were not willing.'
Jesus Christ
Matthew 23:37

This book was presented to:

....

with much love from:

....

On:

....

Pray for the peace of Jerusalem: 'May those who love you be secure. May there be peace within your walls and security within your citadels.' For the sake of my brothers and friends I will say, 'Peace be within you.' Psalm 122:6-8

Jesus rode into Jerusalem on the back of a young donkey.

Crowds joined the procession.

Palm tree branches and cloaks were placed on the road.

The crowd shouted out, "Hosanna to the Son of David."

In the temple at Jerusalem Jesus chased away the greedy men who used the temple as a trading place.

Jesus was pleased to hear the children singing praises and cheering.

He made the blind people see and the lame people walk.

Jesus sent two of his disciples to get ready for the Passover Feast. They were to meet in the upstairs room of a house in Jerusalem.

Jesus and the rest of the disciples joined them in the evening. At the supper, Jesus said, "This bread is my body. This wine is my blood. Remember me when you eat and drink."
This was the first 'Lord's Supper'.

Followers of Jesus all over the world still remember him in this way today.

Jesus and his disciples went to the Garden of Gethsemane.

Jesus asked Peter, James and John to keep him company while he prayed but they fell asleep.

Judas came up to Jesus and kissed him - not as a sign of friendship. This was a sign of betrayal - pointing out Jesus to the wicked men who wanted to arrest him.

Jesus was led away to the high priest's house.

Jesus was let down by Peter too.

While Jesus was in the high priest's house being questioned, Peter stayed outside in the courtyard. Three times someone asked him if he knew Jesus and three times he denied it.

The cockrel crowed at day break. Jesus looked at Peter. How ashamed Peter felt.

He was oppressed
and afflicted,
yet he did not open his mouth;
he was led like a lamb
to the slaughter,
and as a sheep
before her shearers
is silent,
so he did not open his mouth.
By oppression
and judgement
he was taken away.
Isaiah 53:7-8

Early in the morning,
all the chief priests and
the elders of the people
came to the decision
to put Jesus to death.
They bound him,
led him away
and handed him
to Pilate, the governor.
Matthew 27:1-2

When he was accused
by the chief priests
and the elders,
he gave no answer.
Matthew 27:12

Jesus was sent to Pilate the Roman Governor who could find no fault with him - then to Herod, where he was cruelly mocked - then back to Pilate.

Pilate suggested that Jesus could be released, but the crowd shouted "No. Release Barabbas."
"Crucify him! Crucify him!"

Jesus was led away to be crucified - nailed to a wooden cross.

Jesus was not angry. He showed love to his enemies.
He prayed to God: "Father forgive them, for they do not realise
what they are doing."

Jesus asked his friend John to look after his mother Mary.

Two thieves were crucified along with Jesus.
One of them knew he was a sinner and realised that Jesus
was the Saviour.
"Remember me when you come to your kingdom" he asked.

Jesus gave him far more
"Today you will be with me in Paradise," he promised.

He was assigned
a grave with the wicked
and with the rich in his death,
though he had done no violence,
nor was any deceit in his mouth.
Isaiah 53:9

...He was numbered
with the transgressors.
Isaiah 53:12

Two robbers were crucified with him,
one on his right
and one on his left.
Matthew 27:38

Now there was a man named Joseph,
a member of the Council,
a good and upright man,...
Going to Pilate,
he asked for Jesus' body.
Then he took it down,
wrapped it in linen cloth
and placed it in a tomb cut in the rock,
one in which no-one had yet been laid.
Luke 23:50; 52-54

From 12 noon till 3 o'clock there was darkness over the land as Jesus was bearing the punishment for sin.
"Why have you left me alone?" he called to God.

As he died the big curtain of the temple was torn in two; the rocks were split open by an earthquake.

When the soldiers saw these miraculous signs they said "This was certainly the Son of God".

Joseph and Nicodemus took Jesus' body from the cross, wrapped it in linen and placed it in a tomb in a garden.

A big stone was placed at the entrance of the tomb, sealed securely. A guard was set to keep watch.

Early in the morning on the first day of the week (Sunday) some ladies came to the tomb. They wanted to anoint Jesus' body with spices.

When they reached the tomb, they found the stone rolled away and an angel sitting on it. Inside were two other angels.

"Do not be afraid. Jesus is not here. He is risen from the dead."

...My tongue sticks to the roof of my mouth;
you lay me in the dust of death.
Dogs have surrounded me;
a band of evil men has encircled me,
they have pierced my hands and my feet.
I can count all my bones;
people stare and gloat over me.
They divide my garments among them
and cast lots for my clothing.
Psalm 22:15-18

When the soldiers crucified Jesus,
they took his clothes,
dividing them into four shares,
one for each of them,
with the undergarment remaining.
This garment was seamless,
woven in one piece from top to bottom.
"Let's not tear it," they said to one another.
"Let's decide by lot who will get it."
This happened that the scripture might be fulfilled
which said, 'They divided my garments among them
and cast lots for my clothing.'
John 19:23-24.

**M**ary Magdelene was weeping in the garden because she did not know what had happened to Jesus.

A man, whom she thought to be the gardener, spoke her name, "Mary!"

She immediately realised that he was Jesus.
She ran with the good news to the disciples.

Jesus appeared to the other disciples too.

Cleopas and his friend were walking back home to Emmaus. A stranger came along side and talked with them. He explained what had happened to Jesus from the Old Testament.

Not until supper time did they realise that the stranger was in fact Jesus. Jesus asked for a blessing on the food and then he disappeared.

"The Lord really has risen," they declared.

Seven of the disciples went fishing on the sea of Galilee - with no success.

The man standing on the beach told them to put the net down again. Then they caught a huge number of fish.

John recognised Jesus "It is the Lord" he said. Peter immediately jumped out of the boat and ran up to meet Jesus.

They had a lovely breakfast of bread and fish.

W hen they were at the Mount of Olives, Jesus told his disciples that they would be his witnesses at home and in many parts of the world.

As he blessed them, he was lifted up into heaven, right through the clouds.

The discipes stood gazing up to the sky where Jesus had gone.

Then, two men in white clothes told the disciples "In the same way as you have seen Jesus being taken up to heaven, he will return one day."

This filled the disciples with joy.

They went to work preaching the good news everywhere they went.   We should pass on this good news too.

It was the Lord's will
to crush him
and cause him to suffer...
After the suffering of his soul,
he will see the light of life
and be satisfied;
by his knowledge my righteous servant
will justify many,
and he will bear their iniquities.
Therefore I will give him a portion
among the great,
and he will divide the spoils
with the strong,
because he poured out his life unto death.
Isaiah 53:10-12

At the ninth hour Jesus cried out in a loud voice, ...
'My God, my God, why have you forsaken me?'
Mark 15:34

On the first day of the week,
very early in the morning,
the women took the spices they had prepared
and went to the tomb... suddenly two men in clothes
that gleamed like lightening stood beside them. ...
'Why do you look for the living among the dead?
He is not here; he has risen!
Remember how he told you,
while he was still with you in Galilee:
"The Son of Man must be delivered
into the hands of sinful men,
be crucified and on the third day be raised again."
Then they remembered his words.
Luke 24:1 ; 4-8

The story doesn't end in Jerusalem though. The story continues and lasts for ever. It is the story of the Kingdom of God. Jesus Christ once said, 'A time is coming when you will worship God neither here, nor in Jerusalem.' He knew the important place wasn't Jerusalem. He knew that one day all the old things would pass away and everything would be made new. The Lord's people will one day worship him in a new place, a perfect place. Heaven will be their home.

When you give your life to Jesus Christ you are made into a new creation. This is when you become part of God's kingdom and the story continues in you…